AMAZING SPACE

SPACE ROVERS

BY LORI DITTMER

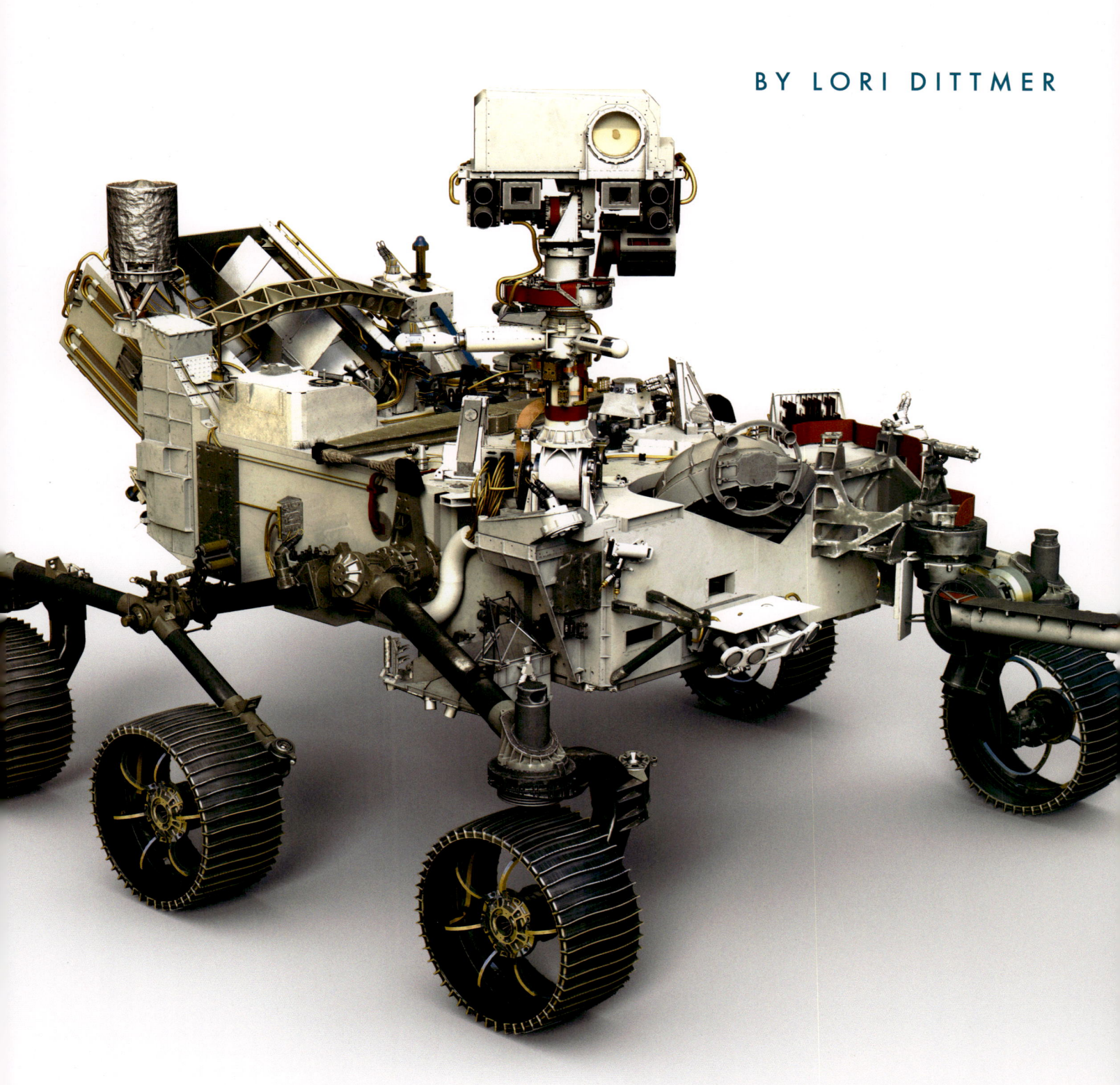

CREATIVE EDUCATION • CREATIVE PAPERBACKS

Published by Creative Education and Creative Paperbacks
P.O. Box 227, Mankato, Minnesota 56002
Creative Education and Creative Paperbacks
are imprints of The Creative Company
www.thecreativecompany.us

Design by The Design Lab
Art direction by Graham Morgan
Edited by Ana Brauer

Photographs by TK NASA/NASA/Joel Kowsky, 16, NASA/
JPL, 8, NASA/JPL, 9, 18, NASA/JPL-Caltech, 5, 14, 17, 20,
22, NASA/JPL-Caltech/Malin Space Science Systems, 2,
NASA/JPL-Caltech/MSSS, 13, 21; Wikimedia Commons/
Unknown, 7, Armael, 6, NASA/JPL-Caltech, cover, 1, NASA/
JPL-Caltech, 10

Library of Congress Cataloging-in-Publication Data
Names: Dittmer, Lori, author.
Title: Space rovers / by Lori Dittmer.
Other titles: Amazing space (Creative Education, Inc.
(Mankato, Minn.))
Description: Mankato, Minnesota : Creative Education and
   Creative Paperbacks, [2025] | Series: Amazing space |
   Includes bibliographical references and index. | Audience:
   Ages 6–9 | Audience: Grades 2–3 |Summary: "Learn
   about space rovers and how the robotic machines aid in
   research. This astronomy title for elementary-aged kids
   includes captions, on-page definitions, a space science
   feature, additional STEM resources, and an index"—
   Provided by publisher.
Identifiers: LCCN 2024018569 (print) | LCCN 2024018570
   (ebook) | ISBN   9798889892335 (library binding) | ISBN
   9781682775998 (paperback) | ISBN   9798889893448
   (ebook)
Subjects: LCSH: Roving vehicles (Astronautics)—Juvenile
   literature. Classification: LCC TL475 .D58 2025 (print)
   | LCC TL475 (ebook) | DDC   629.2/95—dc23/
   eng/20240513
LC record available at https://lccn.loc.gov/2024018569
LC ebook record available at https://lccn.loc.
   gov/2024018570

Printed in China

Table of Contents

Space rovers are robots.

They move on the surface of moons and planets. Scientists control them from Earth. Rovers have equipment to take pictures. They take soil samples. Then, they send information back to Earth. They help us explore outer space!

As of 2024, six rovers have been sent to Mars and seven to the Moon.

In the 1970s, the Soviet space program sent two small rovers to the Moon. They were called *Lunokhod 1* and *Lunokhod 2*. Scientists used a remote control to operate them from Earth. The rovers sent thousands of pictures from the Moon.

Lunokhod is Russian for Moonwalker.

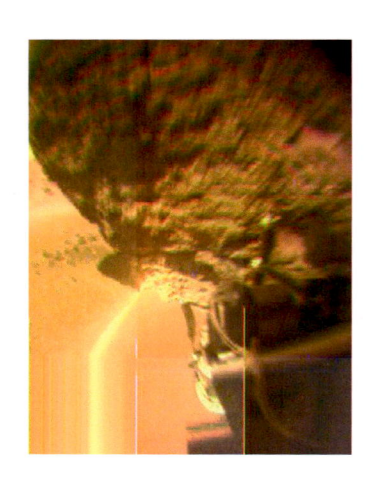

Image taken by Sojourner on Mars.

NASA has sent five rovers to Mars. The first, *Sojourner*, landed in 1997. It was about the size of a microwave. The rover took over 500 pictures. Three months later, NASA lost contact with it.

NASA The National Aeronautics and Space Administration is a U.S. agency that explores space

After that, scientists built bigger rovers. They lasted longer and sent back more information. Two rovers landed on Mars in 2004. *Spirit* was active until 2010. *Opportunity* ran until 2018. In 2011, NASA launched *Curiosity*. In 2021, *Perseverance* landed on Mars. Both rovers are still active as of 2024.

Perseverance is about the size of a car.

A rover is powered by a battery. The brain of a rover is a computer system. This system sends information to Earth. Metal legs connect wheels to the body. Thick treads pull the wheels over bumps and dips.

Many rovers were named by students who had entered naming contests.

A rover has a camera attached to its neck. This gives it a higher view of the area. A rover reaches out an arm. The arm holds another camera or a different tool. Sensors gather data about the air and soil.

Perseverance has a microphone to record sounds on Mars.

Scientists pack rovers into a spacecraft. They blast the rovers into space with a rocket. The trip to Mars takes about seven months. The rover lands with a parachute. Small landing rockets keep it from crashing. Now it is ready to roll!

An artist's concept drawing of Perseverance landing on Mars.

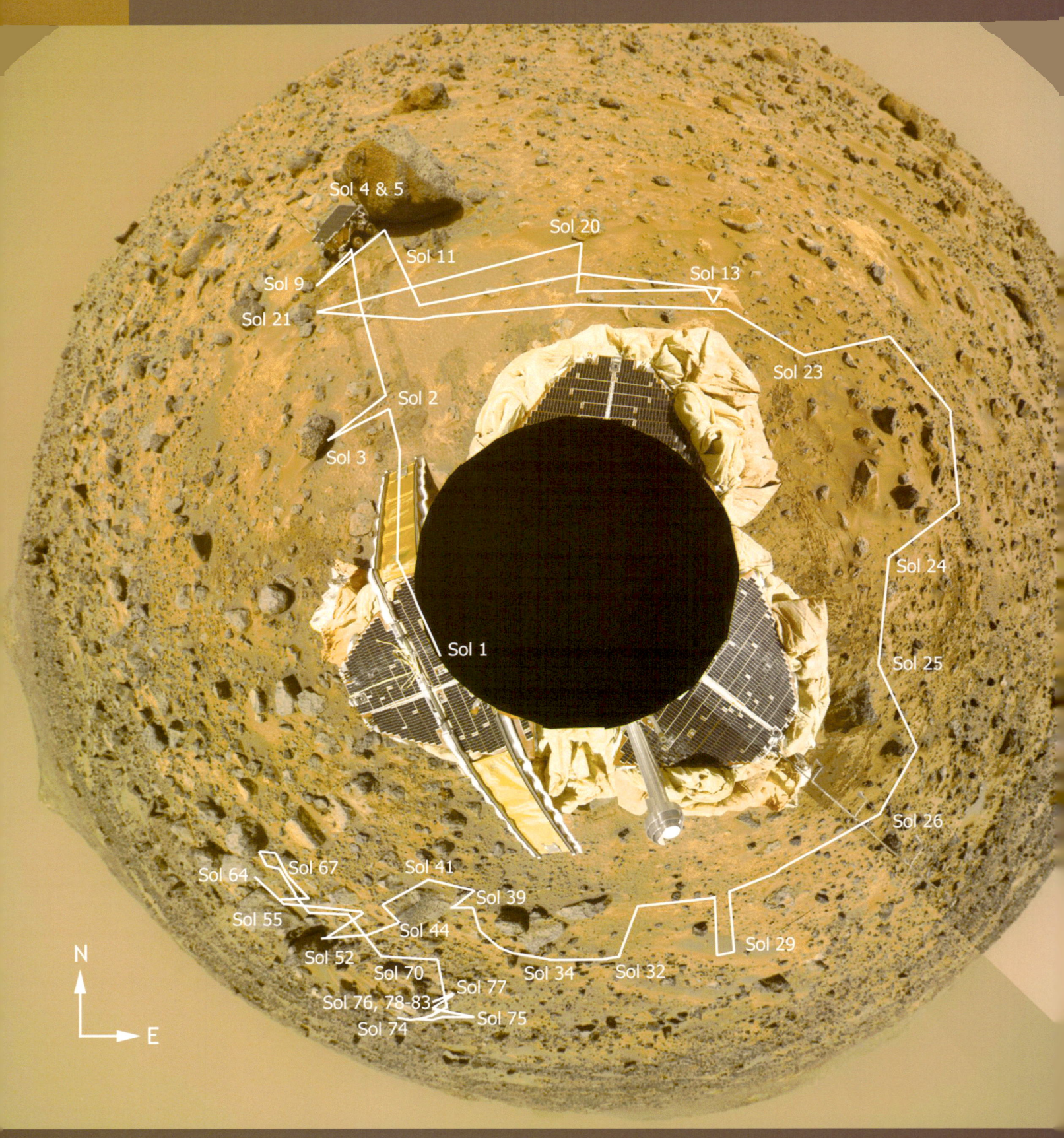

Sol 4 & 5

Sol 20

Sol 11

Sol 13

Sol 9

Sol 21

Sol 23

Sol 2

Sol 3

Sol 24

Sol 25

Sol 1

Sol 26

Sol 64

Sol 67

Sol 41

Sol 39

Sol 55

Sol 44

Sol 29

Sol 52

Sol 70

Sol 34

Sol 32

N

E

Sol 77

Sol 76, 78-83

Sol 75

Sol 74

Scientists on Earth look through the rover's camera view. They send computer commands telling the rover where to go. The rover makes a map of the safest path. When it gets to a new location, it sends a "postcard" of where it ended up.

As of January 2024, Curiosity had traveled 19 miles (31 km) on Mars.

The first observation of a target selected by Opportunity using a software called AEGIS.

Space rovers have given us a lot of information. Pictures show us what Mars looks like. Air and soil samples help scientists plan for the future. We have a better idea about what to expect when humans visit Mars.

In 2025, scientists plan to send three rovers to the Moon to explore the surface.

Spotlight: Perseverance

The *Perseverance* rover, nicknamed Percy, landed on Mars in 2021. It carried a helicopter drone called *Ingenuity.* The drone showed scientists the best place to send Percy. The rover moves slower than a person walks. It can tilt without tipping over. It drills into rocks with a long arm. Percy has collected more than 20 chalk-sized samples of rock. A future mission will send the samples back to Earth.

Read More

Finan, Catherine C. *Space Machines*. Minneapolis: Bearport Publishing, 2022.

Goldstein, Margaret J. *Landing on Mars*. Lerner Publications, 2024.

Murray, Julie. *Rovers*. Minneapolis: Abdo, 2020.

Websites

FunKids: Landing a Rover on Mars
https://www.funkidslive.com/learn/deep-space-high/destination-mars/landing-mars-rover/
Watch a video about how a rover lands on Mars.

Kiddle: Lunar Roving Vehicle Facts for Kids
https://kids.kiddle.co/Lunar_Roving_Vehicle
Read more about the rovers sent to the Moon.

Note: Every effort has been made to ensure that the websites listed above are suitable for children, that they have educational value, and that they contain no inappropriate material. However, because of the nature of the Internet, it is impossible to guarantee that these sites will remain active indefinitely or that their contents will not be altered.

Index